Exam Facts

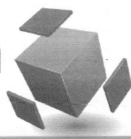

SERIES 99

Operations Professional Exam

Study Guide

Derek Bryan

MW01240988

OPERATIONS PROFESSIONAL EXAMINIATION
Series 99 Exam Facts

By David Bryan
First Edition
© Exam Facts
Http:\\www.examfacts.com
U.S.A

Table of Contents

Series 99 – Operations Professional Examination

Pass the Series 99 Operations Professional Exam by using Exam Facts "Just the Facts" study guide.

The purpose of the Operations Professional Qualification Examination is to provide reasonable assurance that certain operations personnel associated with a FINRA member, "covered persons" as defined by FINRA Rule 1230, understand their professional responsibilities, including key regulatory and control themes, as well as the importance of identifying and escalating regulatory red flags that may harm a firm, its customers, the integrity of the marketplace or the public.

Welcome

Thank you for choosing Exam Facts Series 99 Study Guide, First Edition. This book is part of a family of premium-quality Exam Facts books, all of which are written by outstanding authors who combine teaching experience with real life working experience.

Our goal is to bring you the best books available to help you succeed. I hope you see all that reflected in these pages. We would be very interested to hear your comments and get your input on how we can improve our products. Feel free to let me know what you think about this book or any other Exam Facts book by sending us an email at support@examfacts.com. If you think you've found a technical error in this book, please let us know and we will definitely research and correct it. Your response is critical to our efforts at here at Exam Facts.

Thank you,
Colton McGovney,
Chief Editor at Exam Facts.

About The Author

Derek Bryan was a former accountant who had a strong passion for the Financial Markets. He shifted his focus to become a successful Financial Analyst and now uses his experience and background to teach many on the rules and regulations of Finance as an independent consultant. With a strong focus and desire he also is an avid golfer with a low handicap determined to win an amateur golf tournament someday. Derek is committed to provide readers the knowledge for you to be successful. With this edition, future financial candidates can rest assured that they will be receiving the latest study material available to advance their career.

Acknowledgement

Thank you to the many students who helped with our books. Your input is was critical in what we write.

Why Exam Facts?

We create study guides that are compiled facts that you need to know. No fluff, no long stories that can be distracting to what you really need to learn and remember. Some of our guides have questions filtered in but we try to give you facts, straight to the point so you remember and use that information in your deciphering and understanding of the test questions.

Exam Facts gets some of the best experts in each field to compile and write what is needed for you to be successful. We also get input from you, the test taker on what you'd like to see or if all possible, what we have missed.

We also strive to keep the price as low as possible, sometimes even a hundred dollars cheaper than other guides on the market.

Exam Information

Series 99 – Operations Professional Exam

Exam Info:

Time Limit:	150 minutes
Cost:	$125 US as of December 2012. Note that this is the examination enrollment fee ONLY--other fees may also apply. Please visit the FINRA Registration/Exam Fee Schedule for more information.
Number of Questions:	110 (10 are not scored)
Passing Score:	68%
Format:	Multiple Choice
Prerequisites:	See Finra.org
Exam Date(s):	Any weekday
Exam Locations:	Find your U.S. or international exam center here
Official Exam Website:	http://www.finra.org

Just the Facts

Series 99

SERIES 99

When was NYSE was founded?
1792

Define the Securities Act of 1933
Covered new issue in primary markets; IPOS; Full Disclosure; Prospectus; Red Herring

Define the Securities Act of 1934
Covered trading in secondary markets. Formed the SEC; Antifraud Rules; Margin: Regulation T; Registers People (Exchanges, Firms, Individuals).

Define the Maloney Act of 1938
Enabled the creation of non-exchange SROs.

Define the Item
Date/Number

Define the NASD
Created in 1938 for NASD to act as SRO for OTC market.

Define the Trust Indenture Act of 1939
Added security for Bond investors which requires and agreement (indenture) between the issuing corporation and the trustee who acts on the behalf of the bond owners.

Define the "The Investment Company Act of 1940"
Covers companies that formed to pool investor's money, e.g., Open-end Investment companies called Mutual Funds; More than 100 shareholders; Minimum $100,000 in assets; Annual reports to SEC; Semiannual reports to Shareholders.

Define the "The Investment Advisors Act of 1940"
Regulate firms that sell their investment advice for a fee; includes managers of Wrap accounts where a single fee is paid for investment

advice and transaction costs; ABC Test (Advice, Business, Compensation).

Define the SIPA - Securities Investor Protection Act of 1970
Covers industry funded insurance which covers the customers of BDs (Brokers /Dealers) where a BD might go bankrupt; $500,000 coverage per Separate Customer; $250,000 limitation on Cash Coverage; Industry-Funded; Not part of U.S. government.

Define the ERISA - Employee Retirement Income Security Act of 1974
Provides standards for funding, vesting, fiduciary responsibilities of pension and 401(K) plans.

Define the MSRB (Municipal Securities Rulemaking Board) of 1975
To write rules and regulation for the municipal markets.

Define the Insider Trading Act of 1988 (ITSFEA)
In response to 1980 scandals of Insider Trading of material and non-public information. No penalties existed before; now (a) Criminal from DOJ - $5mm fines and/or 20 years imprisonment; (b) Civil from SEC - Treble (3x) damages on amount gained or loss avoided; disgorgement of profits; covers both Tippers and Tippees - any person can be violated of this law; (c) Bounties - May not exceed 10% of the penalty.

Define the TCPA - Federal Telephone Consumer Protection Act of 1991
Discourage cold callings of consumers and those who calls must maintain a Do NOT Call list. Can call only from 8 am to 9 pm in customer time zone

Define the Penny Stock Rule of 1991
Defined Penny Stocks to be less than $5 and requires a firm to have a signed disco lure document from buyers stating they understand the risks.

Define the "The USA Patriot Act of 2001"
Covers Anti-Money Laundering
CTRs: $10,000 Currency Transaction Reports ...
SARs: Suspicious Activity Report ...
CIP Procedures

Define the FINRA
Created in 2007 by merging NYSE and NASD regulatory functions.
FINRA is the primary SRO for the securities industry.

Define the Balance sheet has to be created before filing for IPO registration
90 days

Define the Disclose share ownership of offers and underwritings as part of pre-filing in IPO
If they own at least 10% of the securities

Define the IPO cooling off period after registration process
20 days

Define the Effective Date in IPO
20 days after the last amendment in response to a deficiency letter as part of the IPO

Define the Public Offering Price (POP) in IPO
Set in the morning of the effective date and also called the Post Effective Date

Define the Accredited Investor
Net worth $1,000,000.
Individual gross income of $200,000; joint $300,000

Define the Regulation D Private Placement securities may NOT be sold to

More than 35 Non-Accredited Investors

Define the Lock-Up period before Securities from pre-IPO investors, private placement buyers, etc., can be sold

6 months

Define the Restricted Securities Rule 144

Holding Period
(1) 6 months - no resale ...
(2) 6 months to 1 year - volume restriction (maximum of 1% of total outstanding shares OR the average weekly trading volume of the past 4 weeks ...
(3) After 1 year - no restrictions

Define the Rule 147 for exemption of securities sold within the borders of one state

(1) 80% of gross revenue from that state
(2) 80% of assets located within that state ...
(3) 80% proceeds used to expand facilities within that state ...
(4) 100% of the purchasers are principal residents of the state.

Define the Non-branch Location

A temporary location for securities business for less than 30 business days in any calendar year

Define the inspection requirements of the OSJ (Office of Supervisory Jurisdiction) ...

Annually

Define the inspection requirements of the Non-OSJ Branch that supervises other locations ...

Annually

Define the inspection requirements of the Non-OSJ Branch with no supervisory functions ...
Every 3 years

Define the inspection requirements of the Nonbranch Location ...
Periodically

Define the inspection requirements of the Personal Residence
Periodically

Define the inspection requirements of the SRO rule for trade subject to investigation
(1) Written statement to SRO within 1 week after completion of investigation
(2) A written statement of the firm's finding by the 15th of the month following the calendar quarter of the trade ...
(3) Statement must be filed even if no disciplinary action was taken by the firm

How long are communications approved by FINRA to be kept in a file for?
3 years after the last date of use

Correspondence to more than 25 people in a 30 calendar day period used to promote a product or financial recommendations then what?
Principal must approve it as a correspondence is subject to review but needs no FINRA approval

Customer complaints to be kept at each office of Supervisory Jurisdiction in a file for how long?
4 years

Customer complaints to be reported to FINRA how long?
10 business days of learning it

Customer complaints Summaries must be sent to FINRA in what time frame?
on a quarterly basis
due on 15th of month following the end of the calendar quarter

FINRA must be notified if a person is involved in a civil litigation that resulted in an award or settlement of how much?
> $15,000

Same as above but for an associated person of the member firm involving suspension, termination, disciplinary actions with fines in excess of how much?
$2,500

Advertisements and Sales Literature must be approved in writing by a Principal and kept for how long?
The last 3 years as well as kept in a readily accessible location for the first 2 years

Sales Literature (Group correspondence)
No FINRA filing; Keep records for 3 years

General Sales Literature and Advertisement
File with FINRA for 1 year; Keep records for 3 years

Investment Co. Sales Literature and Advertisement
Within 10 Business days after use; Keep records for 3 years

Options Advertisements
10 Business days prior to use; Keep records for 3 years

CMO Advertisements
10 Business days prior to use; Keep records for 3 years

Preapproved Sales Literature
No need if preapproved; Keep records for 3 years

Institutional Sales Literature and Correspondence
No need if preapproved; Keep records for 3 years

BCP (Business Continuity Plan) must be reviewed
Annually

FINRA says that BCP plan must mention what number of emergency contacts minimally?
2 (1 person must be a member of Senior management and Registered Principal).

FINRA retains jurisdiction of a registered person (Form U4) for how long?
2 years; if person leaves the industry and comes back in 2 years then no need to re-register

When a RR leaves the firm the firm is required to notify FINRA in what time period?
30 days via Form U5

Central Registration Depository (CRD) that reviews Form U4 has Broker Check system that maintains employment history of what?

10 years for each broker; involved in Civil settlement of $10,000 or more; sales violation damages of $5,000 or more filed with the last 24 months.

Negative events about a person after post hiring should be reported to FINRA what time frame?
No later than 30 calendar days from discovery

If a person of a FINRA member firm is subject to action by a State or Federal Securities, Insurance or Commodities regulator (SD - Statutorily Disqualified Employee) in what time frame?
Within 10 Business days.

The Regulatory Element of the Continuing Education of a RR requirements RR to take training in what time frame?
2nd anniversary of their registration and then every 3 years after. FINRA will notify the RR 30 days before the anniversary date and RR has 120 days to complete the training. RRs doing military service are exempted from this.

For Accounts that purchase IPOs (new Issues) a member firm that sells the new Issues must do what?
Re-verify account eligibility every 12 months and must retain all copies for at least 3 years.

For an IPO an immediate family member would be considered a Restricted person if what?
The employee gives/receives material support to/from the immediate family member where Material Support is defined as providing 25% of the person's income or living in the same household as the person associated with the member firm

A person is considered restricted if he/she owns how much percentage of the Brokerage firm?
10%

Member firm personnel may NOT give a gift exceeding what about?
$100 per recipient; legitimate business expenses are exempted so
long the gift giver attend that event

Political contributes by members are limited to how much?
$250 per candidate per election (Primary and General elections are
separate events) and a violation occurs if the person cannot vote (out-
of-state) for that official. Penalty is 2 years of prohibition from
engaging in municipal securities business.

How many reports to MSRB on Political Contributions should be sent
2 copies to be sent to MSRB on Form G-37/G-38 by the last day of the
month following the end of each calendar quarter

Define the Issued Stock - Treasury Stock
Outstanding Stocks

Dividends are typically paid when?
Quarterly

Define the Current Yield = Dividend Yield = Annual Dividend Yield
(Quarterly Dividend * 4) / (Current Market Price for a share)

Define the Par value of a Stock
$100

Define the Par value of a Bond
$1,000

Define the 3 types of Derivatives covered
Rights, Warrants, Options

Each stockholder receives what number of rights for 1 common stock held?
1 right

Rights are valid for how long?
Limited period; usually weeks or months

Warrants are valid for how long?
Number of years; some are perpetual

Options are valid for how long?
Limited period till expiry; fixed lifespan

Option Premium how long?
Intrinsic Value + Time Value

Most bonds are issued in multiples of what?
$1,000

Bonds pay interests usually when?
Twice a year (semiannually); typically paid on the 1st OR 15th of the month

Define the Long/short coupon
First coupon is for more than 6 months is a long couple; else short coupon

Bonds settle in how long?
T+3 business days

Interest on Bonds is calculated based on what?
30 days a month on a basis of 360 days a year

Define the Accrued Interest Rate
(Principal * Rate * Days of Interest) / 360

Interest on Treasury Bonds and Treasury Notes are calculated based on what?
Actual days per month on a basis of 365 days a year

When are Zero coupon Bonds paid?
At maturity

Define the credit risk of a U.S. Government security
Virtually zero risk of defaulting as the government has the ability to print money and collect taxes

Define the Investment Grade Bond Ratings
Stops at Medium Grade (Baa from Moody and BBB from S&P)

Define the Speculative/Junk Grade Bond Ratings
Starts at Ba and BB

Define the price of a Bond is expressed in terms of points
Each point is equal to 1% of the bond's part value, or $10. So 90 points = $900.

As interest rate increases what happens?
Price of bond decreases (and vice versa)

Define the 3 different ways of calculating a Bond Yield
Nominal Yield, Current Yield, Yield to Maturity

Define the Nominal Yield
Same as the coupon rate

Define the Current Yield
(Annual Interest Rate) / (Market Price)

The way the Investment Companies are organized and operated is governed by what?
The Investment Company Act of 1940; registration required for more than 100 shareholders and fund must have a net worth of $100,000

Mutual Funds (MFs) provide tax summaries to shareholders when?
Annually

MFs send detailed financial reports to shareholders when?
Semiannually

Define the POP (Public Offering Price)
= NAV + Sales Charge

Define the NAV
= (Total Net Assets) / (# of Shares Outstanding)

Define the Maximum Sales Charge PERMITTED per FINRA Rule
8.50%

Define the Class B Shares charges Contingent Deferred Sales Charge
If held less than 6 to 8 years

Define the Class C Shares

an up-front sales charge of usually 1% and an annual fee of usually 1% of the fund's assets and also may pay a contingent deferred sales charge if he shares are sold in less than 12 to 18 months.

Define the LOI (Letter of Intent) for applying for BreakPoints in Sales Charge
Pledge must be met in 13 months and letter of intent can be back-dated 90 days

Define the UITs (Unit Investment Trusts) are generally sold to investors in minimum denominations of
$1,000

Define the REITs (Real Estate Investment Trusts) have a favorable tax treatment if
90% of the ordinary income generated from the portfolio is distributed to the investors; at least 95% of gross income must be dividends, interest and rents from real property; at least 75% of gross income must be real property income; no more than 30% of the gross income may come from the sale or disposition of stock or securities held for less than 12 months

Define the 3 important types of client accounts
Cash, Margin, Options

When buying stocks in a margin account the customer has to pay at least what?
50% of the purchase and BD will finance the rest

When opening an Options account client has to sign the form and return it to the broker in what time frame?
15 days else no new open positions allowed; only closing transactions are allowed.

If a BD sells a penny stock as of the e last trading day of any month then the BD must do what?
Provide a Monthly statement to the customer that includes the shares and the estimated market value of each penny stock

Penny stock exemptions on disclosure exists when?
If the transaction is with an owner who owns 5% of the penny stock; transactions by BDs whose commissions and markups from penny stock do not exceed 5% of its total commissions and markups.

An established Customer for a BD dealing in penny stock is what?
Customer has account for one year or has made 3 purchases of penny stocks from 3 different issues on 3 separate days.

Each Discretionary order must be approved by a principal when?
Promptly on the day of the trade.

Each Discretionary account must be reviewed for churning when?
Frequently

Not-held orders (Time and Price Discretion) is limited to when?
the trading day (Not-held orders are NOT discretionary orders!)

Not-held orders over 1 day what happens?
client must give RR written permission

CTRs (Currency Transaction Reports) must be filed for all cash transactions by a single customer during what time period?
1 business day that exceeds $10,000, in aggregate

CMIR (International Transportation of Currency or Monetary Instruments) must be filed whenever anyone physically transports,

sends, or receives cash, cash equivalents, or monetary instruments in an aggregate amount of more than what amount?
$10,000 into or out of the United States

BDs who transfer or transmit funds (wire transfers) must collect information about any transfer of what amount?
$3,000 or more

SARs (Suspicious Activity Reports) are to be filed by BDs is to be filed whenever a transaction or group of transactions equals or exceeds what amount?
$5,000

Independent audit called Stress Test targeted towards AML is to be conducted when?
Annually, unless the BD does not execute transactions for customers or otherwise hold customer accounts (Proprietary Trading firm) - in which case it has to be done every 2 years

The BD must verify the customer's identity for a new account when?
within a REASONABLE period before or after the account is opened OR before the customer is permitted to a transaction in the account.

A BD must maintain records of the Methods used to verify a customer's identity for how long?
5 years following the closing of the new account

If a BD discovers that one of its client is on the C (Office of Foreign Assets Control) (terrorism suspect list) then the BD must do what?
Immediately block ALL transactions and must inform the federal law enforcement authorities

Define the Penalties for AML violation

20 years in prison and fines of $500,000 per transaction or twice the amount of the funds involved, whichever is greater; civil fines are also applicable

Documents on client accounts must be sent to the customer when?
either within 30 days of opening the new account or with the client's next statement

Updates to documents on client accounts must be sent when?
at least every 36 months

Investment objective changes in an account will lead to notification to customers and RRs by what time period?
30 days or the next statement

Change to account name and address must be sent to the RR by what time period?
30 days

Regulation SP(customer and consumer privacy ruling) dictates that BD furnish a privacy notice when?
First when a relationship is established with a consumer or a customer and then updated versions annually

Evidence for appointment of incumbency on an account for an incumbent must be dated no more than how long?
60 days prior to the presentation, with the exception of a list will and testament

Under UGMA the amount of gift to a minor can be what?
Unlimited but after $13,000 taxes apply

Minors who are at least 14 years old may suggest what?

a new custodian to the court

A BD has up to 35 calendar days to do what?
complete delivery of the security for a DVP customer

BDs must provide a Statement of Account to a customer when?
at least quarterly

During Transfer of Accounts what must occur?
The receiving firm must submit the transfer request immediately and the carrying firm must either validate the instructions or take exception with 1 business day. Then within 3 days of validation the carrying party must complete the transfer of the account to the receiving party.

If a nontransferable asset is liquidated, distributions must be made within what time period?
5 business days of the client's liquidation instructions; all orders with the exception of options positions that expire within 7 business days

Residual credits on an account must be transferred within what time period?
6 months

SIPA - Securities Investor Protection Act of 1970, protects customers to what amount?
a maximum of $500,,000 of which $250,0000 may be for cash holdings

Define the Vedic protection limit
$250,000

Define the DTC subsidiaries

10

DTC was established when?
1974

NSCC was crated when?
1976

Each participant submit trade data to the NSCC at what time?
At the end of each day

FICC (Fixed Income Corporation) has what?
2 divisions: Government Securities division and the Mortgage-Backed securities division (MBSD).

Equity Options are typically issued with expirations of up to what time?
9 months

Define the OCC's cutoff time for Options Expiry
At 11:59 pm, Eastern Time (ET), on the Saturday following the 3rd Friday of the expiration month

Customers MUST initiate their right to exercise by when?
5:30 pm ET, on the last Business day prior to the above expiration date

An expiring Option will cease Trading when?
The day before expiration at 4 pm ET

Define the Option Trade settles
T+1

Define the exercise of an option, which involves the purchase or sale of stock settles in
T+3 business days

Clearing firms MUST notify each Introducing Firm of the Clearing reports it offers by when?
July 31st, annually

Prime Brokerage customers must maintain a minimum Net Equity of what amount?
$500,000 unless the account is managed by a registered Investment Advisor (IA) in which case it is $100,000

Short seller is obligated to return the borrowed shares by what time?
No set period so long the account maintains the required minimum Equity

Market orders will get executed when?
Immediately block ALL transactions and must inform the federal law enforcement authorities

If a limit order is not executed end of day then the client will receive what happens?
A nothing-done notification from his firm

Every order is a DAY order unless otherwise specified and subject to market exposure from what time?
9:30 am to 4:00 pm.

What number of market markers are needed for Listing on Nada?
At least 3

Transactions in Nada securities must be reported within what time period?
30 seconds

Many active stocks have what number of Market Makers (MM) ?
More than 50

At what time does BDs have to send information about all its trades to NSCC?
End of day (same day)

Complex transactions that require Comparison (non-electronic) and settled ex-clearing must have Comparisons sent within what time?
1 business day of the trade

For unrecognized trades anytime that a difference is found and subsequently resolved, the party in error should send a corrected confirmation within what time period?
1 Business day

For unrecognized trades (DKs - Don't Know) the party receiving the confirmation needs to notify the confirming party when?
Promptly by Telephone and then within 1 Business day send a written notice with return receipt requested indicating non-recognition of the transaction and then within 4 Business days send the contrabroker a DK notice.

FINRA's markup policy sets up what?
5% guideline that also applies to markups, markdowns and commissions

Payment for Order flow where BD receives payment from a MM must be disclosed to the customer when?
At the time of opening the account and then annually thereafter

Marking the close violation refers to a series of transactions when?
at or near the close of trading, i.e., at or within MINUTES of 4:00 pm

Some firms raise margin requirements at what time?
stock goes to$5 and may even ask for 100% equity

Define the Corporate Securities in Cash or Margin Accounts
Settlement = T+3 Business days; Customer Payment = T+5 Business days

Define the Municipal Securities(Municipal Bonds)
Settlement = T+3 Business days; Customer Payment = Exempt from Reg T

Define the U.S. Government Securities(T-Bills)
Settlement = T+1 Business day; Customer Payment = Exempt from Reg T

Define the Cash
Same day

Define the Option Trades
Settlement = T+1 Business day; Customer Payment = T+5 Business days

FINRA can grant exceptions on delays due to exceptional circumstances but request must be filed with FINRA when?
prior to the REG T deadline and if no extension is granted then the BD is required to SELL out the position and FREEZE the account for 90

days. Customers who pay up in this time period is considered to have reestablished credit and can again be extended normal credit terms.

Firms that transaction in Investment Company Shares must transmit payments received from customers to the Investment Company when?
- By the end of the 3rd Business day following receipt of a customer's order
- By the end of 1 Business day following receipt of customer's payment (whichever is the later date) ...
- If payment is received from yet another BD then within 2 Business days

Variable Contract Payments to the Issuer when?
Promptly

Variable Contract Payments to the Issuer involving wholesale transactions when?
2 Business days

Define the Unit of Delivery for Stock Transactions
100 Shares

Define the Unit of Delivery for Bond Transactions
in $1,000 denominations, but NO denomination larger than $100,000

Cashier's checks usually clear when?
the next day

All checks received by a BD must be what?
Promptly processed; Cashiering Dept. cannot delay processing; BDs may NOT accept post dated checks from clients!

Wire Transfers are viewed as what?
Immediate Funds and no clearing delay

Define the Sell-Out
Selling BD has the right to do this immediately, without notice

Define the Notice of Closeout for a FINRA member that buys in or sells out another member
must notify the other member of such an action on the SAME day

Define the Reg T requires that a trade executing in a Cash account
Must be paid for full within 5 Business days

Define the Reg T requires that a trade executing in a Margin account
50% must be paid within 5 Business days

Define the Margin requirements on Government Securities
1% with less than 1 year of maturity and a maximum of 6% for scurrilities with 20 years or more to maturity (both initial and maintenance requirements)

Define the Margin requirements on Municipal Securities
7% of the market value

Define the Margin requirements on Corporate Bonds
Investment Grade: 10% of the market value
Non-Investment Grade: Max Of (20% of market value, 7% of Principal Amount)

Define the Margin requirements on Convertible Corporate Bonds
50% of the market price of the Bond

Define the Margin requirements on Arbitrage Positions
- If long a security that is convertible into an equal number of shares of a short position then 10% of the market value of the long position
- If client is long and short an equal number of shares then it is equal to 5% of the long position

Define the Margin requirements on Options
100% (as a wasting asset, options have no loan value)

Define the Margin requirements on New Issues (IPOs)
Investor has to wait 30 days to purchase a primary offering on margin

Define the Margin Loan Consent Agreement changes
Must be sent to clients at least 30 days prior to the changes.

Define the Margin Disclosure Document to be sent to clients
At the time of opening the account and then annually thereafter. Also needs 30 days advance written notice prior to change.

Define the Amount that may be Re-hypothecated
The Customer Protection Rule permits BDs to use stock with a value of 140% of the customer's debit balance as a Collateral for a Bank loan. This 140% applies to the amount of stock that may be used as collateral, not the amount that may be borrowed. The BD is allowed to borrow only the amount that it lent the customer!

Define the Excess Margin Securities are those whose value exceeds
140% of the debit balance (loan amount) of a customer.

When a BD lends stock to another BD the lender has the right to do what?
recall the stock at any time.

When a BD lends stock to another BD the borrower can do what?
has to deposit the full market value of the stock at the time of the
loan and NOT the Reg T requirement

The minimum initial deposit for a short position is what?
MinOf($2000, 100% of the purchase price)

**Define the maintenance requirement for a LONG margin stock
position**
25%

**Define the SMA (Special Memorandum Account) will be credit with
dividends**
100%

A Margin Account becomes RESTRICTED when what?
the Equity falls below the 50% Reg T requirement but is still greater
than the 25% minimum maintenance requirement.

Define the For Sales in a Restricted Account
An amount equal to only 50% of the sale is credited to SMA and may
be withdrawn by the customer. If the withdrawal causes the account
equity to fall below the maintenance requirement, the account is now
a Phantom SMA.

Prior to effecting a short sale, per REG SHO, a BD must do what?
locate securities that can be used for delivery by Settlement Date
(SD).

Easy to Borrow list must be less than what?
24 hours old and provide reasonable grounds for belief that a security
on the list will be available to be borrowed.

If a person does not deliver the borrowed security within 35 days what happens?
the BD that effected the transaction must borrow the security or buy a security that is in like kind and quantity to close out the position.

A Threshold security is put on the threshold securities list if there is an aggregate fail to deliver position for what?
for 5 consecutive settlement days at a clear firm for 10,000 shares or more AND equal to at least 0.5% of the total outstanding shares of the issuer.

Per REG SHO, a BD that fails to deliver position at a clearing firm in a THRESHOLD SECURITY for a what?
continuous period of 13 settlement days or 35 consecutive settlement days then the BD must close out the fail to delivery IMMEDIATELY, by purchasing securities of like kind and quantity.

Per SEC Rule 204 (Close-out Requirements) a BD that have a fail to deliver by Settlement date is required to do what?
IMMEDIATELY (beginning of T+4 trading day) purchase or borrow the security to close out the fail. If not compliant then NO short shares on this security is permitted by the BD. This rule applies to ALL securities, whereas the 13-settlement-day rule applies to THRESHOLD securities only.

Define the minimum initial deposit for a short position
Min Of($2000, Reg T which is 50%)

Define the maintenance requirement for a SHORT margin stock position
generally, 30%.

Define the Maintenance requirements on Leveraged ETFs

Multiply by leverage factor: For a double long portfolio it is 2x25%; for a triple short portfolio it is 3x30%.

Define the Margin Disclosure Document updates
Must be sent to clients at least 30 days prior to the changes.

A pattern day trader is a customer who day-trades is when?
4 or more times in a 5 Business day period.

Pattern day trader have a minimum initial equity requirement of what?
$25,000 (instead of the $2,000). This minimum must be deposited in the account before any day-trading begins!

Day-Trading buying power is limited to what?
4 times the trader's maintenance margin excess, determined as of the close of the previous day.

If a day trader exceeds her buying power limitations then she must do what?
must meet a day-trading margin call within 5 Business days.

If margin call is not met within 5 business days for a day trader then what happens?
Trading in the account is restricted to a cash-available basis for 90 days or until the call is met.

Funds deposited in Day-trading account to meet the minimum equity requirements or a day-trading margin call must do what?
remain on deposit in the account for at least 2 business days.

DTC reconciliation is done when?

each day between what the firm believes is held at DTC and the actual quantity on deposit at DTC.

A BD is required to maintain physical possession or control of all fully paid and excess margin securities that belong to its customers when?
Promptly

Special Reserve Account (SRA) computations must be made when?
Weekly as of the close of the last business day of the week and the deposit must be made no later than 1 hour after the opening of banking business on the 2nd business day following the determination.

If a BD fails to make the required deposit in the Reserve Bank Account within 1 hour after the opening of banking business on the 2nd day following the computation then what happens?
The BD must notify the SEC by telegram immediately and must follow up by a notification in writing. This notice must also be sent to the BD's Designated Examining Authority.

Clients receive Free Credit Balance Statements when?
at least quarterly

Box counts of physical examination and a count of all securities must be made when?
at least once in each calendar quarter

During a Box Count the BD must verify the status of all securities subject to its control but NOT in its physical possession, such as securities in transfer or in transit, where this situation has existed for what time?
more than 30 days.

A BD must record on its books and records all security differences that are unresolved when?
not later than 7 business days after the security count.

A short securities difference is subject to a partial net capital deduction (a haircut) after when?
7 Business Days

A full haircut arising for a short securities differences is done when?
if unresolved after 28 Business days.

If securities are missing but no criminal activity is suspected, reports must be submitted to the SIC (Securities Information Center) and the Transfer Agent within what time period?
2 business days of discovery (1 Business day after a 2 day search).

If securities are missing as a result of an internal audit and criminal activity is not suspected, a report must be filed when?
no later than 10 business days after discovery.

If securities are suspected to be Stolen or Counterfeit then when?
report to FBI, SIC and Transfer agent within 1 Business day of discovery.

If securities that were reported lost or stolen are subsequently recovered then a notice must be sent to the SIC and to FBI, if applicable when?
within 1 Business day of recovery

FINRA member firms are required to send Balance Sheets of Financial Condition Disclosure to customers when?
Every 6 months.

FINRA member s are required to carry a Blanket Fidelity Bond covering officers and employees for loss of fidelity (misplacement, forgery, securities loss, fraudulent trading, etc., coverage should be what?
25000 for EACH SECTION of the bond
If net capital is less than $600,00 then 120% of the requirement ...
If net capital greater than $1 million then $5 million

FINRA member firms must review their Fidelity Bond coverage when?
Annually, as of the anniversary date of the issuance of the bond.

Any adjustment required in the amount of the Fidelity Bond must be when?
made within 60 days of the Anniversary date of issuance.

Member firms must notify FINRA if any Fidelity Bond is cancelled, terminated or substantially modified
within 10 Business days.

The date a Dividend is authorized is know as the what?
Declaration Date.

Dividends are usually paid when?
Quarterly

Dividends are taxable when?
the year in which they are paid/received.

The Ex-Dividend date (ex-date) is typically done when?
the 2nd Business day prior to the Record Date.

The Ex-Dividend date is set by whom?

the SROs, e.g., FINRA

On the Ex-Dividend date the stock price will be what?
Reduced by an amount equal to the dividend to be paid

A buyer can still obtain the dividend after the normal ex-date when?
by purchasing the security in cash up to and including the record date.

SEC Rule 10b-17 requires Issuers of Securities to report to FINRA (not the SEC) all dividends and other distributions when?
at least 10 days prior to the Record Date.

The majority of Bonds pay Interest when?
Semiannually

Some securities like GNMA pass-through certificates pay Interest when?
Monthly

Callable Bonds often contain a restriction on how soon the call feature can be exercised, which is typically how long?
5 to 10 years from the date of the issue.

Blotters are created on what day?
a trade-day basis with all transactions being posted no later than the next Business day.

A supervisor is required to review each account to make sure it is current and accurate when?
as frequently as necessary but at least monthly.

General ledger items must be updated when?

at least monthly.

Items to the general ledger must be posted when?
within 10 Business days of the month's end.

Suspense accounts used to post problem items not yet resolved must have the word "suspense" included in the title of the accounts and the records must be kept for how long?
a period of not less than 6 years.

All records created by a BD must be kept in an easily accessible place for how long?
first 2 years of their existence.

Partnership articles (BD organized as a Partnership) and articles of incorporation, minute books and stock certificate books (BD organized as a Corporation) must be maintained for how long?
the Lifetime of the firm.

Fail to receive, fail to deliver how long?
Posted no later than 2 Business days after the SD (Settlement) Date

Long and short stock record difference how long?
Posted no later than 7 Business days after the discovery

Securities in Transfer, Dividends, Interest Received, securities borrowed and loaned, monies borrowed and loaned when?
Posted no later than 2 Business days after the date of the securities or monies involved

Define the Order Ticket
Prepared before the execution of the transaction

Define the Confirmation, Comparisons
No later than the Business day after the transaction

Define the Option Record
No later than the Business day after the Option was written

Define the WSP (Written Supervisory Procedures)
Former version must be retained when updating

Define the Associated person's application
Prepared prior at or prior to the beginning of employment

Define the Record Types that must be maintained for 6 YEARS
Posting Requirements

Blotters are created when?
Must reflect transactions as of the trade date and must be prepared no later than the following Business day.

Define the General Ledger
Must be posted as frequently as is necessary to determine compliance with the Net Capital Rule, but NOT less frequently than once per month.

Define the Customer Account Ledger
Posted no later than the Settlement Date

Define the Position Record
No later than the Business day after the SD of the date of Securities movement

Define the Cash and Margin Account Records
Must be prepared before the execution of a transaction

If a firm decides to use a form of electronic storage media other than the Optical Disk Technology then the firm must notify its DEA when?
at least 90 days prior to the using the other method.

A firm that uses micrographic or electronic storage media must have a place where the SEC and its SRO can review stored files when?
Immediately

If a BD fails to maintain Books and Records (Noncurrent Books and Records) then it must give notice to the SEC and its DEA when?
that very day and must file a report within 48 hours detailing steps being taken to correct the situation. This report must be transmitted by overnight delivery.

Define the Type of Broker-Dealer (BD) & Minimum Dollar of Net Capital

Carrying Firm
$250,000

Prime Broker
$1,500,000

Firm-Commitment-Underwriters
$100,000

Market Makers (MMs)
$100,000

Introducing Firm (fully disclosed basis to another firm)

$5,000

Introducing Firm (fully disclosed that receive customer securities)
$50,000

Mutual Fund Firms
$5,000

M&A Firms
$5,000

For a Carrying BD the FOCUS (Financial and Operational) Combined Uniform Single) Report Part I must be filed when?
Monthly, within 10 Business days of month-end.

For a Carrying BD the FOCUS Report Part II must be filed when?
Quarterly, within 17 Business days of the end of the quarter.

For a non-carrying broker dealer the Focus Part I is NOT required and the FOCUS Part IIA must be filed when?
Quarterly, within 17 Business days of the end of the quarter.

The ANNUAL financial report must be filed when?
no later than 60 days after the date of the financial statement.

Member firms are required to send Balance Sheets to Customers when?
Every 6 months.

Audited Annual statements must be sent to Customers when?
within 45 days after the BD files its annual report with the SEC.

BD should advise customers regarding their Free Credit Balances when?
Quarterly

Members are required to maintain a separate file of all written complaints in each office of Supervisory Jurisdiction when?
for 4 years (increased previously from 3 years).

Customer complaints can trigger a requirement for the member firm to report the event to FINRA when?
within 10 Business days.

Such an event of customer complaint for civil litigation involves when?
a person involved in an award or settlement of more than $15,000 OR $25,000 if a member firm is involved.

Such an event of customer complaint for a member firm withholding of commissions or imposition of fines in excess of what amount?
$25,000

Statistical and Summary information about customer Complaints must be provided to FINRA when?
on a quarterly basis
due on 15th of month following the end of the calendar quarter

Firms must maintain a file containing all Approved Communications for how long?
3 years after the last date of use and also 2 years in a readily accessible location.

Syndicate Records must be kept for how long?
a minimum of 3 years.

If a Syndicate Member, other than the manager, effects a transaction , the firm is required to notify the manager when?
within 3 Business days of effecting the transaction.

Research Records must be created when?
within 30 days after each calendar quarter in which its Research Analysts make a public appearance.

A BD who does not obtain the certifications regarding public appearances must do what?
for the next 120 days disclose, in all research reports prepared by the analyst that the analyst did not provide certifications regarding public appearances.

Time synchronization is done when?
on a daily basis before the market opens and must be within 3 seconds of the NIST (National Institute of Standards Technology) standard. And must be recorded for OATS in military format.

OATS reports must be transmitted when?
on the same day that the order was received or the day that such information first becomes available.

Confirmations are given to the clients when?
after the trade is executed in printed paper or delivered electronically

BDs are required to provide customers with a statement of account when?
at least quarterly; usual practice is to send it monthly in any account in which there was activity.

Upon written instructions from a customer, a BD may hold up a client's mail for what time period?
up to 2 months for domestic travel and up to 3 months for travelling abroad.

BDs are required to provide a consolidated Form 1099 for Tax Records to the customers and this form is typically generated when?
by Feb 15 for the prior tax year.

An Investment Advise Brochure that n contains information about its background and business practices must be delivered to clients and prospective clients what happen?
no less than 48 hours prior to entering into a written or oral advisory contract (Exemptions: Investment Company clients or contracts requirement payment of less than $200.)

Investment Advisers often generate independent performance reports when?
On a Quarterly basis

Mutual Finds must send detailed Financial Reports to their Shareholders when?
at least twice a year; The Semiannual report and the annual report.

For prohibited transactions in an ERISA (Employee Retirement Income Security Act) account the IRS may impose what?
a 15% excise tax.

ERISA standard age for coverage is what?
21 years or older and have worked for the employer for at least 2 years (one year for the 401(k) plans).

ERISA standard for vesting schedule is what?

fully vested after 5 years or they must be 20% vested after 3 years and fully vested after 7 years of service.

The maximum annual, tax-deferred contribution that employees may make to a 401(k) is what?
$17,000 ($16,500 in 2011).

Employees age 50 and above may contribute up to what amount?
$22,500 ($22,000 in 2011).

Define the Retirement Plan Type & Contribution Limit

Profit Sharing
25% of employee's salary

410(k)
$17,000

Keogh (HR-10)
MinOf($50,000, 20% of self-employed income is deductible)

Traditional IRA
$5,000 or $10,000 if nonworking spouse

Roth IRA
$5,000 or $10,000 if nonworking spouse for income less than $110,000

SEP IRA
Employer: 25% of employee's salary OR $50,000, whichever is less

SIMPLE (Savings Incentive Match Plan for Employees) IRA
Deferrals limited to no more than $11,500 indexed for inflation);
employer matches dollar for dollar up to 3% of pay

403(b)/457 Plans
$17,000 (Typically the same as 401(k) plans)

Define the Penalty for withdrawal prior to 59.5 years in 401(k), Keogh, IRAs
10% (not applicable for 457 plan) and the amount withdrawn will be
added to the taxable income if the plan was tax deferred

Define the distributions in Keogh (HR-10) plans
begin by April 1 of the year following the later of (a) the calendar year
in which the employee turns 70.5 years, or (b) the calendar year in
which the employee retires.

IRA contributions for any given year must be made by the deadline for filing income tax returns for that year
April 15th

I Define the RA investors can withdraw money without paying penalty
if they are under the age of 59.5 and restricted to $10,000 for the
purchase of a home for the first time or the account owner becomes
disabled or the money is used to pay for medical expenses not
covered by insurance or medical insurance premiums when the owner
is unemployed.

Define the Under the RMDs (Required Minimum Distribution) clause Investors who have not begun withdrawals from their Traditional IRAs
by the age of 70.5 years may also incur a tax penalty.

Define the Roth IRA investors may perform early withdrawal without paying penalties

if the owner is 50.5 years or older or becomes disabled or money used for purchase of a first home or money is used to cover certain medical expenses or medical insurance premiums or for qualified higher education expenses.

Define the A parent, grandparent, or complete strange, which adjusted gross income is within certain limits may contribute to the ESA (Coverdell Educating Savings Account) Plan

a maximum of $2,000 per year to the account. (The total from various people cannot exceed $2,000 during any given year).

If money in ESA is not withdrawn, then what?

by 30th birthday then it is subject o ordinary income taxes plus a 10% penalty.

Define the 529 Plan contributions

limited to $13,000 to avoid the gift tax rule but depends on state laws

An Annuity contract owner who withdraws from an annuity when?

before the age of 50.5 years may be required to pay a tax penalty

For Mutual Funds the FINRA rules specify a maximum sales charge of what?

8.5% (NOTE: No such maximum sales charge on a Variable Annuity).

In an Annuity the Annuitant receives payments for how long?

Life

For a Variable Product a FINRA Member must transmit all Applications and Premium Payments to the Issuer (Insurance company issuing the contract) when?

Promptly

To determine the suitability of a Variable Annuity the BD has
up to 7 Business days from receipt of the application package to make
the determination

1035 Exchanges which are contracts funded with existing client asset transfers by RRs are often viewed as inappropriate if what?
if the client has made another 1035 deferred Variable Annuity
transfer with the prior 36 months.

In a Limited Partnership, General Partners (GPs) must contribute how much?
at least 1% to the capital.

The maximum underwriting compensation for a public IPO is what?
10% of the gross dollar amount sold

Any change to a customer's account information must be what?
must be requested from the client in writing

Define the Regulatory Element
required within 120 days of the second anniversary of an
individual's registration and every three years thereafter

Define the Firm Element
required annually

Define the Suspicious Activity Report (SAR)
Customers engaging in suspicious behavior. Examples include:a.
Customer makes daily deposits designed to avoid the Currency
Transaction Report (CTR)

reporting requirements (e.g. frequent deposits of $9,000).
b. Small business accounts that deposits funds and then quickly wires those funds to seemingly
unrelated accounts.

Define the Currency Transaction Report (CTR)
Over 10,000

Define the Gifts
limited to $100 per recipient per year. Reporting requirements - all gifts must be recorded

Define the NAV
company's total assets minus its total liabilities

Define the (T+3)
Equities, Corp Bonds, Municipal Bonds, US Govt Agencies

Define the (T+1)
Treasury Securities, Listed Options

Define the National Securities Clearing Corporation (NSCC).
clears trades of 1) equities and 2) corporate bonds

Who must sign the FOCUS report?
i. The CEO,
ii. The CFO (FINOP), and
iii. the COO

FOCUS report Part I Monthly Carrying firms when?

10 business days after the end of each month.

FOCUS report Part II Quarterly Carrying Firms when?
17 business days after the end of each month

Bond prices and interest rates have what?
an inverse relationship.

Long term bonds are more sensitive what?
than short term bonds

Low coupon bonds are more sensitive what?
than high coupon bonds.

Define the long-term zero coupon bond
very, very sensitive to interest rate changes.

Equity options settle for what?
the actual underlying securities.

ACATS allows what?
customers to transfer accounts from one broker-dealer to another

Deposit/ Withdrawal at Custodian (DWAC) requires what?
Securities Transfer Agents Medallion Program (STAMP)

Direct Registration System (DRS) allows what?
shareholders to maintain their securities directly on the books and records of the issuer. No Stamp REQUIRED

Equities trades are reported when?
within 30 seconds

Define the Reg T initial margin requirement
50%

Define the Maintenance margin requirement in a long margin account
25%

Define the Maintenance margin requirement in a short margin account
30%

Define the Insider trading penalties-Civil
Three times the profits gained or losses avoided

Define the Insider trading penalties-Criminal
Fines up to $5 million and up to 20 years in prison

Define the agent that may only share commissions with
other FINRA registered personnel.

Define the Restricted Stock
Unregistered securities
Example: Reg. D private
placement, Restrictive legend, Sales-Holding period
Six months, and
Public companies, SEC Notice None required

Define the Control Stock

Owned by corporate insider
Example: Officer, Director, 10% or
more shareholder, Owner's account indicates insider
status. Sales--Volume limits - Greater of:
1% of the outstanding shares being
sold, or
Average reported weekly trading
volume during the four weeks
preceding the sale.
Frequency - maximum over 90 days. SEC Notice-Form 144 Prior to sale
customer transfer or deposits physical certificates ensure that the
certificates are in good form by checking the certificates against the
Lost and Stolen
Securities Program (LSSP) to ensure the certificates were not stolen or
counterfeit

Define the Cumulative preferred stock

all current and past-due preferred dividends must be paid before any
dividends can be distributed to common stockholders

Define the Participating preferred stock

the preferred shareholder can receive additional dividends if a
predetermined condition is met (example: if the dividends for
common shares exceeds that of the preferred shares, the preferred
shareholders will receive an additional dividend.)

Define the Convertible preferred stock

Preferred stock that allows the shareholder to convert the preferred
shares into a fixed number of common shares

How long do you keep: Advertising/sales literature?

3 Years

How long do you keep: Customer Trade Confirms?
3 Years

How long do you keep: Form U4/U5?
3 Years

How long do you keep: Fingerprint records?
3 Years

How long do you keep: Customer complaints?
4 Years

How long do you keep: Anti-money Laundering Records?
5 Years

How long do you keep: Customer New Account Forms?
6 Years

How long do you keep: General Ledgers? Purchase/Sales Ledgers?
6 Years

How long do you keep: Partnership Articles?
Lifetime

How long do you keep: Articles of incorporation?
Lifetime

How long do you keep: Form BD?
Lifetime

How long must records be easily accessible?
2 Years

Is electronic storage permissible?
Yes, with notice to FINRA

Cashiering Dept. Functions

Define the Regular Way
Most securities settle on a regular-way basis, which refers to the normal number of days to complete the transaction. This number varies depending on the security involved. For corporate stocks and bonds and municipal securities, the settlement for a regular-way transaction is three business days after the trade date (T + 3). For Treasury securities and options, settlement occurs one business day after the trade date (T + 1) .

Define the Special Settlement
If either party seeks to alter the timing of settlement on a particular trade, the adjusted period must be agreed to prior to the transaction. For example, if a stock seller is in urgent need of funds and needs a next-day settlement (vs. T + 3), the buyer must agree to these conditions prior to the transaction and may offer a slightly lower price for the shares.

Define the Seller's Option
When the settlement cannot be completed on a regular-way or for-cash basis, the seller may request settlement by a seller's option. At the time of the transaction, both parties to the trade may agree to a seller's option, which gives the selling firm additional time beyond the normal three business days to make good delivery.

Define the Cash Settlement

The settlement is completed on the same day as the trade. This option, which must be agreed to by both parties, can be used for any type of security.

Settlement Dates

Define the Settlement in Foreign Markets
Securities settlements in foreign trading venues do not conform to U.S. standards. Each foreign market has its own settlement cycle and good delivery standards. The DTCC has linkages to many overseas depositories to facilitate international settlements.

Define the Do Not Confuse Customer Payment With Settlement
Do not confuse the customer's obligation with those of the firms involved in a given trade. Regulation T requires that customer payment for purchases in cash and margin accounts be made promptly, which typically means T + 5. In cash accounts, the full purchase price must be paid, whereas in margin accounts, a specified percentage of the purchase price is due.

Settlement versus Customer Payment

Define the Extensions
Under exceptional circumstances, a member firm may apply to FINRA or an exchange for an extension of time for the payment of the amount due. This would apply in such circumstances as a delay in the mails, preventing the customer's payment from being received on time. In this case, an extension could be granted by FINRA or an exchange. The broker-dealer must apply for the extension prior to the Reg T deadline.

Define the Frozen Accounts

What happens if no extension is granted? The broker-dealer is then required to sell out the position and freeze the account for 90 days. This means that the customer must pay for all purchases in advance for the 90-day period. After paying in advance for the 90-day period, the customer is considered to have reestablished credit and may once again be extended normal credit terms.

Define the Exemptions
Reg T may be referred to as the SEC payment cycle on your exam and is found within the 1934 Act. Remember, not all securities are subject to the Act since many are exempt under federal securities laws. Examples of exempt securities include U.S. Treasuries, municipals and short-term commercial paper.

Define the free-riding
The practice of purchasing securities without paying for them in the hope of being able to profit without any outlay of funds is called free-riding and is prohibited under Federal Reserve Board (FRB) rules.

Define the Investment Company Transactions
Firms (including underwriters) engaging in retail transactions involving purchases of investment company shares for their customers must transmit the payments received from the customers to the investment company (or its designated agent):

Define the Variable Contracts
A broker-dealer who sells a variable contract is required to forward the proceeds to the issuer promptly. Underwriting firms engaging in wholesale transactions involving purchases of investment company shares must transmit payments for these shares to the issuer (or its designated agent) by the end of two business days following receipt of payment.

Define the Settlement Methods

Today, this settlement process is generally handled electronically by the DTCC for the majority of securities although some security positions are not DTCC-eligible. Essentially, the DTCC simply adjusts the contra parties' security positions and cash balances on its internal books. The settlement is guaranteed by the DTCC so there is no contra party risk.

Define the DTCC Settlement

Rules for settlement of contracts between member firms fall under FINRA's Uniform Practice Code. Again, settlement occurs on the day in which the buying firm must pay for the securities and the selling firm must deliver them and receive the proceeds from the sale. For example, stock trades done regular-way will settle on the third business day after the trade (T + 3). As noted previously, the DTCC would simply journal the positions and monies from between each clearing firm's account. This process is referred to as book-entry settlement.

Define the Book-Entry Settlement

As mentioned, rather than making physical delivery of securities or cash when settling securities trades, many firms use book-entry settlement. However, if a firm wishes to use book-entry settlement, all transactions in depository-eligible securities must be settled through a registered securities depository such as the National Securities Clearing Corporation, or the Depository Trust and Clearing Corporation. In reality, each firm on a locked in (affirmed) stock trade is actually settling the position with the NSCC, the DTCC subsidiary.

Define the DRS (Direct Registration System)

The Direct Registration System (DRS) is a DTCC service that provides investors with an alternate approach (referred to as a direct registration)to holding their securities as either physical certificates or in street name with their broker-dealer. The system provides for electronic registration of securities in an investor's name on the books for the issuer's transfer agent. The electronic shares can then be quickly transferred between the transfer agent and broker-dealers as needed. Under this system, investors can have their book-entry positions registered directly on the issuer's records and will receive an ownership statement from either the issuer or its transfer ageut. If desired, at a later date the owner can request the position to be transferred electronically to his/her bank or broker-dealer or issued in certificate form.

Define the DWAC (Deposit Withdrawal At Custodian)

The DWAC transaction system is run by the Depository Trust Company and is often used to convert physical certificates into an electronic form or vice-versa. The system permits DTC participants (brokers and custodial banks) to request the electronic movement of positions to or from the issuer's transfer agent. The transfer agent acts as custodian for the shares. Unlike the DRS system, only DTC participants can initiate transactions in the DWAC system. The DTC participant (typically a broker-dealer) places instructions in the system requesting the movement of shares to or from the transfer agent. The transfer agent must then receive confirming instructions from the issuer or shareholder to accept the DWAC.

Define the Repurchase Agreements

In a repurchase agreement (repo), one party sells securities (usually T-bills) to an investor and agrees to repurchase them at a specific time, at a specified price. In effect, the dealer is borrowing funds from an investor and securing the loan with securities (a collateralized loan). The investor (the lender) receives the difference between the purchase price and the resale price of the securities in return for making the loan. The settlement terms (time and price) for both transactions are established ahead of time.

Define the Reverse Repos

If a dealer purchases securities and agrees to sell them back to an investor at a specific date and price, this is known as a reverse repo or matched sale. In this situation, the dealer would lend funds (with securities as collateral) to the investor and earn the difference in sales prices. Many corporations and financial institutions, as well as dealers, engage in repos and reverse repos. Repos and reverse repos are typically short-term, with most being overnight transactions.

Define the CUSIP Numbers

CUSIP numbers are similar to bar codes in a store and are identifying numbers assigned to each maturity of an issue, and are intended to help in the identification and clearance of securities.

Define the Endorsements and Assignments

A customer who sells a security is required to sign the certificate. The usual method of endorsing a stock certificate is to sign the certificate on the back and then mail the certificate to the broker-dealer. In order to safeguard the certificate while it is in the mail, the seller could send the certificate by registered mail. An alternate method is for the customer to send the certificate, unsigned, in one envelope and to send a signed stock power in a separate envelope. In this way, if the certificate were to fall into unauthorized hands, it would have no value since it would not be negotiable.

Define the Proper Endorsements

Certificates must be endorsed exactly as they are registered.

Define the Medallion Guarantee

Assignments on a security must be exactly as the name appears on the certificate, without an alteration or enlargements of any kind. In addition, the assignment must be guaranteed (a signature guarantee) by a member firm of the NYSE or by a commercial bank. The transfer agent will not accept a security for transfer without a proper assignment and guarantee. This process, known as a medallion signature guarantee, means that the transferring broker-dealer assumes liability in the event of forgery. This guarantee protects customers against unauthorized transfers and also limits the liability of the transfer agent.

Define the Additional Documentation

If an account is registered in the name of an executor or guardian and the security is signed by the executor or guardian, the transfer agent will accept the stock without requiring additional documentation. Transfer agents will not accept a security that was signed by a person

who is now deceased. They will transfer the security only if it is signed by a duly designated executor and accompanied by the necessary legal documents. The documents that are usually required are a copy of the death certificate, an appointment of executor, state tax waivers, and an affidavit of
domicile.

Define the Unit Delivery - Stock Transactions

On stock transactions, deliveries may be for multiples of 100 shares. For example, on a transaction involving 500 shares, one certificate for 500 shares, or five certificates for 100 shares each, or two certificates for 200 shares and one certificate for 100 shares would all be good delivery as these are multiples of 100 shares. However, multiples that are not 100 shares, such as two certificates for 250 shares each, or one certificate for 450 shares and one certificate for 50 shares, are not good delivery.

Define the Mutilated Certificates and Coupons

Mutilated certificates will not constitute good delivery unless validated by the trustee, registrar, transfer agent, paying agent, or the issuer of the securities or by an authorized agent or official of the issuer. A certit1cate is deemed mutilated if anyone of the following elements cannot be ascertained.

• Name of the issuer

• Par value

• Signature

• Coupon rate

• Maturity date

• Seal of the issuer

• Certificate number

Define the Coupons
All physical coupons that have not yet been paid must be delivered with the bond certificate. These include missed payments from issuers in default.

Define the Called Bonds
Bonds that are called prior to the trade date are not good delivery unless identified as called at the time of the trade. If a trade is effected between two dealers and the securities subject to that trade are called in part after the trade date but before the delivery date, then this will not constitute good delivery. If an in-whole call is published between the trade date and the delivery date, this would be good delivery.

Define the Legal Opinions
Delivery of certificates without legal opinions or other documents legally required to accompany the certificates will not constitute good delivery unless identified as ex-legal at the time of the trade.

Define the Insured Securities
Delivery of certificates for securities traded as insured securities must be accompanied by evidence that they are insured. This evidence could be imprinted on or attached to the certificate.

Define the Gifted Securities
An owner of securities may decide to donate the asset to a charity. The donor may use two methods to transfer the securities to a charity. If the stock is held by a broker-dealer and is registered in street name, the client would provide written instructions to indicate his intention to transfer the securities to the charity. A transfer instruction form can be submitted for account title changes and gifting. The signature of the donor (or donors) is required. If the stock is held in the name of the donor, the stock certificate may be

endorsed or the donor will deliver the certificates with a signed stock power.

Define the Restricted Securities

Securities carrying a restrictive legend are not considered to be in good delivery form. Generally these certificates must have the legend removed, which is the responsibility of the selling firm's legal department. Only a transfer agent may remove a restrictive legend. The transfer agent will not remove the legend unless the client has obtained the consent of the issuer in the form of an opinion letter that comes from the issuer's counsel. This letter gives the transfer agent authority to remove the restrictive legend.

Define the Payment and Receipt of Funds - Issuing Checks

A broker-dealer is required to issue customer checks in numerical sequence and post these disbursements to the blotter. Voided checks must be recorded as well. All checks must be signed in ink and must list the payment amount. Blank checks and post -dated checks may not be issued.

Define the Payment and Receipt of Funds - Personal Checks

The cashiering department must post all checks (or cash) received from customers to the blotter and promptly apply them to the customer's account. No payments may be made against these checks until they have cleared. Generally, checks must be drawn against a bank account that is the property of the broker-dealer customer. Payment with third-party checks is usually not permitted due to AML concerns.

Define the Cashier's Checks

Unlike a personal check, a cashier's check will clear quickly once funds have been verified. These items are treated as guaranteed funds and are usually cleared the next day.

Define the Check Processing

All checks received by a broker-dealer must be promptly processed. The cashiering department is not permitted to delay processing checks in accounts in which funds have not yet cleared. Broker-dealers may NOT accept post-dated checks from clients.

Define the Wire Transfers

Wire transfers are viewed as immediate funds. There is no clearing delay. If a client wants a wire transfer from her brokerage account, she must provide the firm with wiring instructions. These instructions would include

• Name of the receiving bank

• Account to be credited (client's bank account name/number)

• Account to be debited (client's broker-dealer account name/number)

• Transfer amount

Define the Institutional Settlement

Institutions often have differing settlement instructions based on the type or nature of a given transaction. Payment and delivery instructions may differ based on product type or even the venue in which the trade occurred. In these cases, the client must provide standing settlement instructions (SS!) to the broker-dealer that detail all of the various payment or delivery instructions. Often, institutions house these SSIs in a database that executing and clearing firms may access. The SSI may be overridden with written permission from the customer.

Define the Sweeps

Another area handled by the Cashiering Department is the moving (sweeping) of client funds into money-market accounts. If a client sells securities or receives an interest or dividend payment, these credits, generally, are automatically transferred to an interest -bearing account. Conversely, if the client purchases securities, the money market is automatically debited.

Define the Failure to Settle - Buy-In

A buy-in occurs when a selling broker-dealer has failed to make proper delivery to a buying broker-dealer. The buying broker will then purchase the securities in the open market, charging the selling broker-dealer that failed to deliver the difference between the contract price and the buy-in price. A buy-in may not be done sooner than the third business day following the settlement date. The broker to whom delivery is due must send a buy-in notice to the contra broker no later than 12:00 noon two business days before the execution of the proposed buy-in.

Define the Sell-Out

If a selling broker-dealer makes good delivery to a buying broker-dealer and the buying broker-dealer refuses to accept the securities, the selling broker-dealer has the right to sell the securities immediately, without notice, in the open market, and to charge the buying broker-dealer with any loss that has been incurred.

Define the Notice of Closeout

A member that buys in or sells out another member must notify the other member of such action on the same day

Define the Rejection versus Reclamation

Sometimes issues other than nonpayment or non-delivery occur in a settlement process. Perhaps one of the broker-dealers inadvertently delivers the wrong security. If the problem is discovered prior to the acceptance of the delivery, this is known as a rejection.

Abbreviations

ADR/ADS

American Depository Receipt (Share)

AIR

Assumed Interest Rate

AMBAC

AMBAC Indemnity Corporation

AMT

Alternative Minimum Tax

APO

Additional Public Offering

ARS

Auction Rate Securities

BA

Banker's Acceptance

BABs

Built America Bonds

BAN

Bond Anticipation Notes

BD

Broker Dealer

CATS

Certificates of Accrual on Treasury Securities

CD

Certificate of Deposit

CDOS

Collaterized Debt Obligations

CEO

Chief Executive Officer

CIP

Customer Identification Program

CLN

Construction Loan Notes

CMO

Collaterized Mortgage Obligation

CMV

Current Market Value

COD

Cash On Delivery

COP

Code of Procedure

COPs

Certificates of Participation

CPI

Consumer Price Index

CPM

Customer Portfolio Margining

CQS

Consolidated Quotation System

CUSIP

Committee on Uniform Security Identification Procedures

CY

Current Yield

DBCC

District Business Conduct Committee

DEA

Designated Examining Authority

DEA

Designated Examining Authority

DJIA

Dow Jones Industrial Average

DRS

Direct Registration System

DTC

Depository Trust Company

DVP

Delivery Versus Payment

EE

Series EE Savings Bond

ELNs

Equity-Linked Notes

EPS

Earnings per Share

ERISA

Employee Retirement Income Security Act of 1974

ETCs

Equipment Trust Certificates

ETNs

Exchanged-Traded Notes

FAC

face-amount certificate

FCA

Farm Credit Administration

FCS

Farm Credit System

FDIC

Federal Insurance Reserve Corporation

Fed

Federal Reserve System

FFCBs

Federal Farm Credit Banks

FHA

Federal Housing Association

FHLMC

Federal Home Loan Mortgage Corporation

FIFO

First In, First Out

FINRA

Financial Industry Regulatory Authority

FMV

Fair Market Value

FNMA

Federal National Mortgage Association

FOMC

Federal Open Market Committee

FRB

Federal Reserve Bank

GAN

Grant Anticipation Notes

GDP

Gross Domestic Product

GMAC

GENERAL MOTORS ACCEPTANCE CORPORATION

GMCs

Guaranteed Mortgage Certificates

GNMA

Government National Mortgage Association

GO

General Obligation Bond

HH

series HH savings bond

IDB

Industrial Development Revenue Bonds

IDR

Industrial Development Revenue Bonds

IDR/IDB

Industrial Development Revenue Bond

ILN

Index-Linked Note

IOs

Interest Only CMOs

IPO

Initial Public Offering

IRA

Individual Retirement Account

IRC

Internal Revenue Code

IRS

Internal Revenue Service

JTIC

Joint Tenants in Common

JTWROS

Joint Tenants with Right of Survivorship

JTWROS

Joint Tenants With Right Of Survivorship

LIFO

Last In, First Out

LOI

Letter of Intent

MBIA

Municipal Bond Investors' Assurance

MBS

Mortgage Backed Securities

MIG

Moody's Investment Grade

MSRB

Municipal Securities Rulemaking Board

NASD

National Association of Security Dealers, Inc.

Nasdaq

National Association of Security Dealers Automates Quotation System

NAV

Net Asset Value

NCI

Non Conventional Investments

NHA

New Housing Authority Bonds

NIC

Net Interest Cost

NL

No Load

NSCC

National Securities Clearing Corporation

NYSE

New York Stock Exchange

OCC

Options Clearing Corporation

OFAC

Office of Foreign Asset Control

OS

Official Statement

OSJ

Office of Supervisory Jurisdiction

OTC

Over the Counter

PACs

Planned Amortization Class CMOs

PCs

Mortgage Participation Certificates

PE

price-to-earnings ratio

PHA

Public Housing Authority Bonds

POA

Power Of Attorney

POP

Public Offering Price

POs

Principal Only CMOs

PPNs

Principal Protected Notes

PSA

Public Securities Association

RAN

Revenue Anticipation Notes

REIT

Real Estate Investment Trust

RR

Registered Representative

RTRS

Real Time Transaction Reporting System

SAI

Statement of Additional Information

SDN

Specially Designated Nationals

SEC

Securities and Exchange Commission

SEP

Simplified Employee Pension plan

SIPC

Securities Investor Protection Corporation

SLGS

State and Local Government Securities Series

SLMA

Student Loan Marketing Association

SMA

Special Memorandum Account

SRO

self-regulatory organization

STRIPS

Separate Trading of Registered Interest and Principal of Securities

T + 3

trade date plus three business day settlement

TACs

Targeted Amortization Class CMOs

TAN

Tax Anticipation Notes

T-Bills

Treasury Bills

T-Bonds

Treasury Bonds

TCPA

Telephone Consumer Protection Act

TIC

True Interest Cost

TIC

Tenants In Common

TIGRS

Treasury Income Growth Receipts

TIPS

Treasury Inflation Protection Securities

T-Notes

Treasury Notes

TOD

Transfer On Death

TRACE

Trade Reporting and Compliance Engine

TRAN

Tax and Revenue Anticipation Notes

TSA

tax-sheltered annuity

UGMA

Uniform Gift to Minors Act

UGMA/UTMA

Uniform Gift (Transfers) to Minors Act

UIT

Unit Investment Trust

UIT

Unit Investment Trust

UPC

Uniform Practice Code

UTMA

Uniform Transfers to Minors Act

VA

Department of Veteran Affairs

VLI

Variable Life Insurance

VRDOs

Variable Rate Demand Obligations

YLD

Yield

YTC

Yield to Call

YTM

Yield to Maturity

ZR

Zero Coupon

Z-Tranche

Zero-Tranche CMO

Definitions

Aggressive Growth Fund

Equity Category; Portfolio: small cap stocks; maximum capital

appreciation; may employ short-term trading strategies; very volatile;

investors must be risk tolerant (possibly young)

American Depository Receipt

American Depository Shares

Annual return

Holding period return

Ask

Offer

Authorized stock

New stock

B shares

Bank End Load

Back-end sales charge

Contingent deferred sales charge (CDSC)

Balanced Fund

Blended Category; Portfolio: mix of equities and bonds; growth with opportunity for income; portfolio mix usually under tighter constraints than growth & income fund

Bondholder

Creditor

Broker

Agent

Brokerage fee

Sales Charge, Sales Load

Buy

Own, Hold, Purchase, Long

C shares

Level Load

Call Risk

Fixed-Income Securities: Bonds are more likely to be called when rates have dropped, forcing reinvestment of principal at lower rates. Many municipal and corporate bond issues are callable.

Capital Risk

General term for possible loss of money invested. This risk is present in most securities.

Capital Risk

Principal Risk

Class A shares

Front end sales charge, front end load

Contribution

Cost basis

Corporate Charter

Articles of Incorporation

Corporate High Yield Fund

Fixed Income Category; Portfolio: Corporate bonds rate BB/Ba or lower; Higher than normal income with higher than normal default risk; Investor must be able and willing to assume default risk; Also has interest rate risk

Corporate Investment Grade Fund

Fixed Income Category; Portfolio: Corporate bonds rated BBB/Baa or higher; Income with modest credit risk; Dividends are fully taxable; Interest rate risk

Coverdell

Educational IRA

Credit Risk

Fixed-Income Securities: Possiblity that principal or interest will not be paid. Credit risk is usually compared to U.S. Treasuries, which are considered to have none.

Credit risk

Default risk

Currency Risk

Changes in value of a currency versus another currency. Current owners of foreign securities may see a negative impact if foreign currency weakens against their home currency.

Dealer

Principal

Distributor

Wholesaler, sponsor, underwriter

Equity Income Fund

Equity Category; Portfolio: dividend paying equities; safe, consistent income with secondary objective of growth; less volatile than other equity funds

Equity income fund

Growth and income fund

Exchange

Switch

Exchange market

Auction market

Global Fund

Foreign Category; Portfolio: Common stock from inside and outside
the U.S. Capital appreciation in whatever markets look attractive to
manager; Exposure to exchange rate risk and political risk (legislative),
in addition to market risk.

Growth & Income Fund

Blended Category; Portfolio: mix of equities and bonds

Growth Fund

Equity Category; Portfolio: common stock; capital appreciation;
income not a consideration; subject to market fluctuations

Growth Objective

Investment objective for increase in invested capital, primarily
generated through price appreciation. Equity securities (stocks) are
usually used in pursuit of this goal.

Income bond

Adjustment bond

Income Objective

Investment objective for regular production of cash from investments, through dividend or interest payments. Bonds and preferred stocks are often used to produce income.

Index Fund

Equity Category; Portfolio: common stock in same proportions as selected index (e.g. S&P 500) Matches the return of the market; Passively managed; Low expenses and portfolio turnover

Industrial Development Revenue Bond

IDR, IRB, IDRB, AMT bonds, Private activity bonds

Inflationary Risk (Purchasing Power Risk)

Fixed-Income Securities: Rise in general level of prices reduces the value of fixed returns. Some debt investors attempt to reduce this risk in their portfolios through equity investments or investments in gold.

Insider

Control person, affiliate

Interest Rate Risk

Fixed-Income Securities: Possibility that increase in general level of interest rates will drive down prices of existing fixed-income investments. Long-maturity fixed income securities have more of this risk than shorter maturities.

International Fund

Foreign Category; Portfolio: Common stocks from outside of the U.S.;

Capital appreciation in markets that might not follow U.S. market;

Exposure to exchange rate risk and political (legislative) risk, in

addition to market risk.

Investment income

interest & dividends

Keogh Plan

HR-10 Plan

Liquidity Objective

This is a primary need for those who never know when they will need

cash quickly. It is the ability to easily turn an investment into cash

without a big impact on the market for the security. Investment

objective for liquidity often goes hand-in-hand with preservation of

capital. T-notes are very liquid but affected by interest rate swings so

not best for capital preservation. CDs are very good at preserving

capital but may lose interest by liquidating early.

Liquidity Risk

Ability to quickly sell an investment at or near current market price.

Regardless of type, more heavily traded securities are more liquid.

Long

Buy, bought, hold, or own

Market risk

Systematic risk

Market Risk (Systematic Risk)

Possible loss of value due to a broad market decline. For equities, this risk is measured by a statistic called beta.

Money Market Fund

Fixed Income Category; Portfolio: cash equivalents such as T-bills, CDs, commercial paper, BAs; Preservation of Capital; attempts to maintain $1 NAV (not guaranteed); used to park funds while making investment decisions

Municipal Bond Fund

Fixed Income Category; Portfolio: Municipal Bonds; Income that is free from federal, and possibly state income tax; higher the investor's tax bracket, the more beneficial the tax exemption; may have some default risk; interest rate risk

Municipal bonds

Tax-free bonds

Mutual Fund

Open-end management company

Mutual Fund Family

Family of funds, mutual fund complex

Naked

Uncovered

Net yield

After-tax yield

Nominal yield

Coupon, coupon rate, interest

Non-systematic risk

Selection risk, business risk

Opportunity Cost Risk

Loss of income or appreciation because an investment was NOT

made. When making one investment, one always forgoes others that

might have provided a better return.

Outstanding shares

Shares held by the public

Over the counter

OTC, negotiated market

Par value

Face amount, principal

Political Risk (Legislative Risk)

Changes in laws or rules may have negative impact on investments.

The common wisdom is that political risk is high anytime Congres is in

session. This is also used in the context of foreign securities.

Preliminary prospectus

Red Herring

Prepayment Risk

Fixed-Income Securities: Possibility that homeowners will prepay

mortgages more quickly than expected when interest rates fall. This

risk is present in mortgage-backed securities and CMOs.

Preservation of Capital Objective

Investment objective for safety of principal being paramount, in

return for which investor accepts lower returns.

Pre-tax

Tax- deductible

Primary market

New issue market, primary distribution, sold by prospectus only

Progressive tax

Graduated tax, income tax

Property tax

Ad Valorem tax

Purchasing power risk

Inflation risk

Recession

Contraction

Regressive tax

Sales tax, Flat tax

Regulation A

Small offering

Regulation D

Reg D, private placement

Rule 147

Intrastate offering, offer in one state

Sale

Redemption, liquidation

Secondary Market

Where "used" stock trades

Sector Fund

Special Types Category; Portfolio: Common stock from particular

industry (e.g., telecommunications); Provides exposure to selected

industry group without the hassle of individual stock selection by the

investor; Less diversification increases risk if sector suffers downturn.

Securities Act of 1933

Act of '33, Paper Act, Full and Fair Disclosure Act, Prospectus Act

Securities Exchange Act of 1934

Act of '34, Exchange Act, People Act

Sell

Write

Separate account

Sub-account

Short

Borrow, don't own

Special Situation Fund

Special Types Category; Possible large gain if situation plays out as manager predicts; Depends on ability of manager to find special deals; May be less diversified than other funds.

Specific ID method

Versus purchase

Speculation Objective

Investment objective for investors that are willing and able to take considerable risks for the chance to hit a big financial home run.

Speculative bond

High yield, junk bond

Stock

Share, equity

Tax Reduction Objective

Investment objective for high-bracket investors facing a big tax bite on taxable investments may find tax-exempt vehicles produce a better after tax return.

Tax-deferred

Tax "delayed", taxed later

Tax-free

Tax-exempt, not taxable

Timing Risk

Investing in a specific security at an inopportune time. Dollar cost averaging is used to avoid this risk.

Total Return Objective (Growth & Income Objective)

Investment objective for a combination of growth of capital and income, but less of each than investments that focus on just one of those objectives. Dividend-producing stocks, such as blue chips, are one way to go after this objective. Another strategy is a portfolio combining some growth securities and some income securities.

Treasury Stock

Treasury Stock = issued shares - outstanding shares

Unsecured corporate bond

Debenture

US Government Fund

Fixed Income Category; Portfolio: T-bonds, T-notes, T-bills; Income

with no credit risk; may be subject to interest rate risk; the longer

average maturity of the portfolio the greater the interest rate risk

Viatical

Life settlement, sale of life insurance in the secondary market

Yield to Maturity

YTM, basis

Please see HTTP://www.ExamFacts.com for the latest Study
Guides in Finance, Healthcare, Business, Law and Technology.

Development Editor: Stacy Hoffman
Technical Editors: Stacy Hoffman and Tim Hetfield
Production Editor: Colton McGovney
Copy Editor: Kristin Kenney
Editorial Manager: Kirk Stone
Book Designers: Derek Bryan
Proofreader: 3 Point Farms Documentation, Inc.
Project Coordinator: River Kelly
Cover Designer: Colton McGovney
Reviewers: Eric Walton, Jackie Conley,

appropriate per-copy fee to editors@examfacts.com.

Limit of Liability/Disclaimer of Warranty: The publisher and the author make no representations or warranties with respect to the accuracy or completeness of the contents of this work and specifically disclaim all warranties, including without limitation warranties of fitness for a particular purpose. No warranty may be created or extended by sales or promotional materials. The advice and strategies contained herein may not be suitable for every situation. This work is sold with the understanding that the publisher is not engaged in rendering legal, accounting, or other professional services. If professional assistance is required, the services of a competent professional person should be sought. Neither the publisher nor the author shall be liable for damages arising here from. The fact that an organization or Web site is referred to in this work as a citation and/or a potential source of further information does not mean that the author or the publisher endorses the information the organization or Web site may provide or recommendations it may make. Further, readers should be aware that Internet Web sites listed in this work may have changed or disappeared between when this work was written and when it is read.

For general information on our other products and services or to obtain technical support, please contact our Customer Care Department at Support@examfacts.com.

Exam Facts also publishes its books in a variety of electronic formats. Some content that appears in print may not be available in electronic books.

Made in the USA
Lexington, KY
15 November 2013